At the Mercy of Ourselves

Poems by Joe McKenzie

Kansas City Spartan Press Missouri

Spartan Press
Kansas City, MO
spartanpresskc@gmail.com

Copyright © Joe McKenzie, 2019
First Edition 1 3 5 7 9 10 8 6 4 2
ISBN: 978-1-946642-90-5
LCCN: 2018914989

Design, edits and layout: Jason Ryberg
Cover image: Rick Frisbie
Title page image: Jon Lee Grafton
Author photo: Mary Lou McKenzie
All rights reserved. No part of this publication may be reproduced or transmitted in any form or by any means, electronic or mechanical, including photocopying, recording or by info retrieval system, without prior written permission from the author.

Spartan Press would like to thank Prospero's Books, The Fellowship of N-finite Jest, The Prospero Institute of Disquieted P/o/e/t/i/c/s, Will Leathem, Tom Wayne, Jeanette Powers, j. d. tulloch, Jon Lee Grafton, Jason Preu, Mark McClane, Tony Hayden and the whole Osage Arts Community.

Thanks to family who have patiently listened to or heard many of these poems, especially Mary Lou, Scott, Delphine, Kevin and Cassi. Thanks to the staff and patrons of the Salina Public Library who always kept life interesting and inspiring in many ways. Special thanks to Lori Brack, who has tried for years to teach me how to write better poems and to Rick Frisbie for support, inspiration and his amazing cover art.

-JM

CONTENTS

Nothing Good / 1

Listener Request / 3

Without Light / 5

Fish Taco / 6

A Simple Slap / 8

Driving Lesson / 9

Celery / 10

Occasional Wildlife Sighting / 12

One Dog Down / 14

Debbie Has 'im by the Balls / 16

At the Mercy of Ourselves / 17

Spring in a Box / 21

Roadside Pee / 22

Motel Pool Nuns / 24

Waiting 'till They Come Kill Us Again / 25

Children are Dancing / 28

Kathy on the Bus / 29

smoke/blow/flick/walk / 31

Jelly Babies / 32

Savage Beauty / 34

Good Boy / 36

Armed and Dangerous / 37

Dead Poor / 39

Safe Distances / 41

Still Life in Lawn Chair / 43

Dinner Invitation / 45

Oh, Come on / 47

Addicted to Lucinda Williams / 49

6 mi W of Cedar Vale / 51

Happy to be the Dog / 53

If You Only Have One Day / 55

Despite it All / 57

Science Quiz / 58

What We Call a Rose / 60

Asking the Neighbor to Shoot His Own / 62

Arriving at Church an Hour Before God / 64

Belly Crawl / 66

Half Crazy / 68

Blessings / 69

Fingers in the Bowl / 71

Goodwill / 73

Roughed Up / 75

It Doesn't Get Better / 77

Thin Crust / 79

Perishables / 81

Discovery Adventure Wonder / 84

Too Early to Cry / 87

This Song / 89

Our goal should be to live life in radical amazement. . . get up in the morning and look at the world in a way that takes nothing for granted. Everything is phenomenal; everything is incredible; never treat life casually.

-Abraham Joshua Heschel

Nothing Good

> for Helen Levitt, photographer
> *There were boxes in the apartment.*
> *One box was labeled "nothing good."*
> ArtNews, May 2009

After she died, old and without family
we opened windows long shut
and went through her things with what we felt
was appropriate detachment from the emotions
that led to their acquisition, gifts at holidays,
birthdays we imagined as joyous days
full of the moist cake of life
like the days she purchased her closet of shoes
that sat polished and ready
for tomorrow, some still-born in their original box,
favorites bought as reserves and never unpacked
but, she knew they were there waiting
in case she broke a heel
lost a single shoe, the odd OCD worry
of needing just a left or a right to make a pair
and in the kitchen nearly every box and can
expired before her and we tossed it
or packed it away
folded clothes for Goodwill
stacked books and records, trashed a lifetime
of trinkets, memories and assorted junk
until we came to a box taped closed
shoved under the bed and labeled nothing good,
and that made us stop our detached destruction

brew a pot in her Mr. Coffee and speculate
about what she might have chosen
to place in the box
to hide under the bed, and
did she do it all at once, going through her photos
or slowly, over the years, struggling
in weak moments
not to place everything in, or content
that it was just a small box in a long life
and we would all have some not so good stuff
we could never let go of
or it us —
until we finally did.

Listener Request

Someone from Otis, Kansas has requested
an obscure American composer's symphony
written in the dark days after his ex-wife's suicide

and the rest of us NPR listeners on this pleasant
Friday morning are tuned in to these angry strings
and discordant bleak woodwinds as we drive to work

too respectful to push a button to jump stations
as we sit in mournful traffic, glancing about
for other captive listeners, heads bowed,

car windows sealed up against that potent mix
of clean country air which we need more than ever
to offset this slow death dirge, until

across the intersection walks a confident woman
pushing an industrial sized baby stroller
with an alert bright eyed girl in a perfectly

silly hat worn to capture our eyes, to delight
and save us, as she saw everything, sensed
the world as it was, felt a sonic ping for help

bouncing across traffic in search of a seed
of hope, which she couldn't articulate
or even recognize the sound of, but

she knew, somehow, this universe was scraping
bottom again, scratching a new musical void
from a sick screech,

which could have made her scream, but instead,
the child chose love and celebrated with a can't-forget-
it crazy and merciful smile and wave, which obviously

is the joy the composer meant for us to search
for and why the listener from Otis called in to help us
re-discover goodness and appreciate this morning.

Without Light

It's rare now to see a smart woman buy
her first pack of convenience store smokes

walk outside to fumble with packaging
open and litter a desolate parking lot, pull

out her first cigarette, look at it shaking,
feel the white thinness in her fingers

place it between her lips, small tears now
as she tastes it, spits, feels an attack of stupid

as she realizes she is without a light, has second
thoughts, remembers her dying mother sucking

oxygen last night, a desperate look in her eyes
wanting one last smoke, a strong desire for

something familiar to kill her, needing
that feeling again, a final taste of life.

Fish Taco

I'm not alone as I stand in a hungry line
of lunch people waiting for first world fish

tacos cooked in a repurposed ghostbusters truck
operating with a city permit in a parking lot

over the noon hour, with a noisy generator
and fish fumes mixing with clean eco-busses

and urban green space water sprinklers under
a pale spring sky with hopeful hints of fluff baby

clouds floating as happy/fat/silent sky things
over this slow food line of non-starving

consumers grasping smart phones and cash, checking
texts and trashing fantasy spam from imagined lovers

while inching slowly toward locally sourced lettuce
that was mindfully shredded in a home kitchen

by a lovely part time tattooed mother/partner/lover
who listens to a podcast while chopping/dicing/

marinating with love the ingredients I'll be eating
on a bench beside the resident homeless guy

who takes it all in with deep meditative breaths
and smiles the smile of knowing it's all connected -

the fish and clouds, podcast and cheese, lovers, sprigs
of cilantro and the massive yank of tides that pull

us all together, as though we needed to be here,
and then my bench partner hands me a napkin

of recycled paper as I ungracefully lurch forward
to drip pico de gallo on this version of the world.

A Simple Slap

The sound of the slap is classic.
A what-you-would-expect smack
that reverberates one second and
if you listen for it - a hiss of a
sting that lifts off the skin like a
small snake with a self-conscious
lisp, and it takes just a half moment,
a can't take it back now act and it's
over already and the world moves on
to a slightly awkward place between
day and night where no one wants
to be, as though we'll all get through
this, it's not a bomb, no one died
nothing to see here, forget about it
as though the inclination to hit
someone was a slight indiscretion
a slip up, another simple act of
violence amidst a daily onslaught
that has bunkered us safely behind
locked doors and yet, there it is —
a hot red hand shape glowing
where her soft pretty cheek used
to wait to be kissed or caressed,
and even when it fades from face
it will have been absorbed to brain
and remembered as a sudden assault,
a surprise attack, whose furious sound
and pain would never quite go away.

Driving Lesson

The thing about speeding to the liquor store
on a back street with dips, dogs and beer
at dusk, no lights, license or insurance card
hip-hop blasting at atomic decibel levels
windows down for safety

you don't want to be in the backseat
with an underage girl
who snuck out of the house
on a school night to paint her nails black
to match her drunk blond friend

who is driving your car
as though she had reinvented driver's ed
and was giving free lessons
while dancing in the driver's seat
one long arm snaking out the window

and then you're flying out of a dip
everyone screaming above the music
and you catch yourself in the rearview mirror
wide eyed smiling
and to your amazement still alive.

Celery

My dog was the first
in the house to hear
the slow green peel
of celery hued paint
sliding off the walls
to the original oak
baseboard everyone
loved, and his head
perked up, his nose
wrinkled like he could
smell chopped celery
in the kitchen, but he
said nothing, not one
whining plea bark -
like dude, it's so hot,
I think your paint
is peeling, don't you
hear it, doesn't it
bother you it's so hot
in here even the ugly
paint is giving up
committing suicide by
melting in the dining
room, or is it a cruel
conspiracy plan of yours
to not turn on a fan, to
ignore the basic elements
of your home while you
sit reading, which I was

doing, lost in an old issue
of Atlantic again, one
of those serious articles of
life and death I usually
skip, but then I heard a growl
that sounded like - a window
please, open a god damn
window as he tilted his
head slightly to the right
which means I had not
been paying attention and
he was questioning my
intelligence or sanity, I
never read that right, and he
rarely cusses, being a proud
and better breed of dog, but
his furry furled brow meant
that I was such a human idiot
I wouldn't even taste the salt
of foamy ocean waves if they
rolled down the front staircase
to flood the main floor, cold
water up to my bare ankles
as I sloshed through the
house opening windows
turning on ceiling fans and
in the warm kitchen stopping
to fetch my smart dog
a dry treat and fix
a nice tuna salad
for lunch to appease my
sudden craving for celery.

Occasional Wildlife Sighting

I see a red chair in a white room
through a glass wall I drive by
everyday.

They want me to see the red chair.
See it empty.
See red on white in a well lit
Russian winter room as I speed
by glancing left for a quick glimpse
of her watching traffic. But, she's
never there. I've looked. Driving by
at 45 mph, I hope to see her swivel
her head 45 degrees to see me.
She has classic model posture. Seems
sad. Indifferent. No one happy sits
like that for long, but it shows off
her long straight shampoo bright hair.
Each day I see a bit more as I round
the parkway curve on my way to work.

I don't honk. She doesn't wave.
Has never smiled our secret smile.
Like a lot of people, she could be
a mannequin - an escort-like ladyquin
I could install myself, but I'd get
caught by security cameras and
uniformed men watching monitors
who would come to life and say:

hey, look at this nut job, dragging
a body, no wait, that's a mannequin,
Jack, sick, but, she looks good,
almost real. No one sits in that chair
but, we better call it in, write a report.

I'd sit her upright in a blonde wig
long black gown and barefoot,
a calm, yet wild-in-captivity look.
We're not going anywhere anyway.
Her hard face would appear serious
maybe bored to be so alone and stuck
in such a common checking weather/
watching traffic life off the parkway
where perfect trees are more alive
in this view from inside her glass room
as endless cars zip by with distracted
drivers, commuters who do not see us
or small birds in seasonal transitions
migrating to a warm place
just beyond our reach.

One Dog Down

Down to one dog now and he flops
his heart on the porch mid-afternoon
in whimpering dreams, rouses
from memory expecting to see her
nosing the tattered screen door or
noisily lapping the water bowl
dripping through a full toothed grin
they used to share when they teased
each other from pups that they were
just dogs - you're a dog, they said, with
their eyes, with their cold nose, just
dirty dogs, all bark, no bite panting
fur ball rescue dogs whose stark
honest breath cleared rooms
happy dogs whose wagged tails
greeted or knocked things over and
not just cross-bred mutts with dormant
pea brains who might misread
a message and run through yards
and across fields as if on a mission
which they would soon forget and
wander home all mud and hung head
dumb, stuck thick with thistle and
sticker, knowing they would be out-
doors until dry, reliving it all,

each wild dog adventure together, an
on-going pissing contest that ended
when we put her down, leaving
him to wonder if life still had meaning
just one lone dog who looks to me
for an answer and sees the same question.

Debbie has 'im by the balls
Overheard walking on a Florida beach

In Florida, they are talking about Debbie
as they walk the bright morning beach,
serious mother with adult daughter
on sand, beaten gritty and off-white, like
Debbie must be, or him, the women
not even pretending to look for shells
or black shark's teeth, their excuse
for being out of the condo to talk
where no one who knows Debbie
or him will overhear snippets of their struggle
coming out in gasps of winter Gulf waves
flowing with the cold gossip of trouble,
though Debbie, having grabbed on,
may be pleased to have him
where she wants him, squirming, for now,
unaware that mother sees her
squeezing the life out of 'im, remembers
another time, another him, a firm grip, angry
waves crashing below the waist
pulling another marriage under water
years ago and how, when the tide
went out, when the sun shone
on a shell littered, shark tooth beach,
she was the one left alone.

At the Mercy of Ourselves

when it becomes unclear whether God
is still on the job using night-vision goggles
to police a planet

that is out of control
on constant alert
in full riot gear
at war with ourselves
while on fire with prayer,
selling guns at flea markets
waiting for rapture or a sign
we're not alone, but clearly
at the mercy of ourselves

on a planet that is hot, tired and angry
looking for new answers
on billboards, street signs
and in movies showing pretty people
we admire doing stuff we shouldn't
and knowing it's not real
we can't be them in this lifetime
with what we were given, but
not sure what happened
to make us this way

so, we grab at anything,
cling to heroes just to be allowed to stay,

to be on the team, to play the game
or watch and tweet as others play
as we wear their colors and scream
cheer, jump, cry and die with them
just to be accepted as we are,
our face, our color, gender, language,
our people, our place in a world

where God is on coffee break
at Starbucks, chatting up dead angels
even as our time gets away from him
as though he or we are saying
hey, we've got this, no problem
unless we misplace our purpose
misunderstand the plan

or can't seem to even recall
what countries are south of the border
or the new taste of hunger
and who can count the diseases,
the drugs, costs or the real cause

of anything, we are so distracted
by breaking news, disturbed by
the final score of a game, immune
to horror, desensitized to reality
blinded by our need

to dress a certain way
to be someone or someone else
to pretend again and again

to be at peace
to be at one
full of faith and grace and yet
often disappointed with others
or ourselves when we can't pull it off
and no longer know what to believe

when we lose hope in our dreams
not sure what is right
not sure what is real
just a vague awareness of life
circling around us
no longer confident of creation
and that plan
for what we are supposed to do

or where we might find out
as churches go out of business
and schools put out a lesser product
of people, who don't have the answers
or the real reason for war
for conflicts with everything different
that we don't try to understand

including ourselves
our inertia and narrow vision
of such a small piece of the planet

so, when it finally rains on the corn crop
it spoils a summer picnic

or trip to the lake
where we could miss the sound of laughter
or a bouncing beach ball of joy

that might fly our way
and we'd instinctively smack it
to someone else, who passes it on
to a child who laughs, runs and plays

not caring or aware
that this is it, the good life,
just a simple day at the beach
with family and friends
and whatever we make come next

so it comes on us slowly
over years, if at all
that this is it
billions of small lives in days of chance
linked by large and small
by beach balls and wars
families and strangers making it happen
sharing the planet,
creating a life and offering the hope

that we have each other
and together
we are at the mercy of ourselves.

Spring in a Box

Spring arrived in a box this year
just a simple re-usable brown cardboard
square we found waiting on the front porch
when we came home from walking
the big dogs. Spring was a surprise on-line
item, back-ordered and almost forgotten, so we
quick stripped winter - the mittens, squall
jackets and insulated boots as we prepared
to open the box together, to smell green
wonder, see light all bunched up in bubble
wrap and while we don't usually open deliveries
with glasses of chardonnay, this seemed
like that kind of box, marked fragile and
this side up, and after the usual bear of a winter,
we were ready for birds to find their voice, to
sing in this messy month that still ripped
us with impersonal winds, crabby drifts
of dirty snow and news that people
we loved had not made it through the dark
season, so we were peckish little sniffly birds
who needed to be new again, who
wanted to breathe, hop and sing too
feel the pulse of joy in our tiny hearts
and here it was wrapped in a box, ready
to touch with our dry winter fingers of hope
and to taste the fresh promise we remembered
from past years, eager to honor each new day.

Roadside Pee

The first time you pee by the side of the road
as a child standing exposed to the moon,
to truckers and tour buses, to every alien
with a high-powered telescope, or an inter-
planetary hi-def satellite tv package

you hardly think about it, the relief, as they say,
is so real as you tinkle for mom, who made your
dad pull over, just in time, before you had an
accident, so now you feel perfect, so in-tune
with the universe, who knew this was all it took

as you stare pissing into near and distant darkness
like a real-life tasteless concrete suburban water
fountain, and as traffic roars by, your father's
blinkers flash out a coded signal to all that a child
is peeing on the grass again, don't look now, relax,

how much pee could one kid have, we've all done
it and the world may stink, but not from this, and
the gods find a balance in arranging roadside pees
so we don't all have to go at once, creating traffic
snarls and streams of yellow piss in the ditches

but, we've learned to take turns like good kids
and on rainy nights we might learn to hold it,
to squirm, fidget and think of something else,
because sometimes the world does not provide
everyone with a decent place to go, simple as

that seems, but, we all do it, wait our turn,
take a desperate leak out in the universe, safe
under a blanket of winking stars, with the
blessing of mothers, who smile, relieved
we are peeing by the side of the road.

Motel Pool Nuns

You never see a flock of nuns at a motel
pool, but there they were, a miracle in black
one piece convent issued logoed swimsuits,
dark sunglasses hiding their gaze
as they slathered lotion in silence
praying Mother Superior would bless
their tans, might ask to see the white
outline of a crucifix on their holy chests
as these young sisters did not want
to lay out without Jesus
remembering spring breaks in college
when they hit the beach with Mojitos
in their water bottles as a boom box
blasted hip hop and rock back in the day
BC
before daily prayer
before vows
before committing their lives in service
to his name, so even while lounging
at a cheap motel pool, they thanked him
for convent rules that allowed them
freedom to be real, to be women who
praised the sparkling water reflecting his light,
which they were absorbing into beatific smiles
as fingers worked rosaries,
each Hail Mary offered up to a young virgin
who never had a day off at the pool,
so it was the least they could do
on this fine summer day. Amen.

Waiting 'till They Come Kill Us Again

> Words of Former President Hamid Karzai, of Afghanistan
> replayed on the Rush Limbaugh radio show - 9/26/06

We should at least be comfortable while we wait,
not dwell on our first death, bloody details
we would just as soon forget,
the thick smell of life disappearing so quick
bodies leaping from a thousand feet
to escape the fire, the crash of concrete,
ghosts in dust and smoke running in the streets
the sound of our whole world screaming
and then silence, endless moments
of silence strung together forever
but, that was the first death
and now we are waiting, sitting
by a window watching the sky
pacing praying pacing praying
peering through curtains at the pretense
outside on a street of green fertilized fescue
with perfectly straight edging while
inside a tv the size of a football field
displays the news from a Midwestern
face and the voice of a middle-aged mother
of three who is paid millions to smile
and re-assure us that everything is being done
or to frighten us at the exact moment
we thought it was safe to eat dinner
while we wait

like guests at a reality talk show
at which we will utter our last words
approved thoughts and ideas
with heartfelt feeling or enthusiasm,
looking directly into the camera
whose soft red light reminds us that
this moment is LIVE and we are on
the air, smiling and being watched
while we wait for them
to come kill us again,
wondering if they can really do that,
can drive over the border from Canada
in rented family sedans, refill gas tanks,
study a map and review their assignment to kill
us, maybe questioning the fact they've already
blown us up once, years ago, when
these guys were just kids, and wasn't it
New York, or was it Washington, they wonder
and maybe there's been a mistake
to assign them to come back, so
they call in to the office to double-check
their assignment - no,
they wouldn't question that, they might
talk about it as they watch the news lady
smile, listen to the American story -
guns everywhere, shootings every night
the sad crazy Americans killing their police,
fighting each other, waving that flag
so proud of what they fight for,
big, rich people building their walls

but, you could smell fear on the streets
they think, as they watch us and wonder why
so many were sitting at home waiting,
consider the possibility of a trap, of being
caught and have a few laughs about that
as they work their plan, hang out, buy
cigarettes, some wine, meet friends
for a nice dinner at Outback, share family
photos, buy souvenir t-shirts to send back
home to be remembered, like anyone might,
but eventually, they would do what most
would do, follow orders
do the job
and kill us again.

Children are Dancing

Next door to the house where children dance
all night, as if they powered the moon
and stars with glorious incessant energy,

a single white bulb watches beside the ratty
flowered chair, where the wrinkly neighbor
lady sits working her blessed needles knitting

another striped afghan for the church bazaar
that is always bought and given to whoever
is most needy since each skein

of red is woven with prayers for the hungry
green yarn worked through with prayers
for the sick and the blue for the blue

who live in a house that may look like yours
on any normal crazy day when everyone is
somewhere just being busy and will never hear

the color of her old prayers faded to a washed out
teal of lonely years knitting, but brightened by
a jitterbug memory of children dancing with joy

jumping on chairs, sofas and dogs and all the lumpy
beds of every unmade heart up and down this street
whose pulse still beats for you.

Cathy on the Bus

Cathy on the bus with Simon
and Garfunkel pretended to be asleep
when they sang that they were lost and
looking for America - she had awakened
with pain from their diet of Mrs. Wagner's pies
and cigarettes and a headache from staring
through a rainy bus window looking
looking for America, for a real place
that was unlike anything she was seeing
in Ramparts magazine, when she pretended
to read the revolutionary drivel and angst
that had put them on the bus
on this journey to forget
what it's like to be at home
with mom in the kitchen drinking wine,
humming Motown, frosting church cakes,
squeezing out a pink message of *help*
in the frosting, as if Michigan
was a desert island and a cake cutter pilot
would fly over and see the mess
life had become and radio for rescue,
before eating a slice with ice cream,
as if we could have it both ways
to stay in the kitchen for the revolution
to ride the bus, ride forever
to a soundtrack of familiar singable songs
that helped us forget, helped us laugh

and cry, to think we could say
we were still crazy when we weren't,
when we weren't alone in our desperate search
for a version of America,
an old America, a basic black and white
and browning place
we had borrowed and loved for so long,
as if it held the promise of acceptance,
a bright shining light
a wobbly bridge over such a troubled time.

smoke/blow/flick/walk
for Ogden Nash - *I eat my peas with honey.* . . .

when my entire life becomes a moment
I blow smoke hard out my mouth into
thick city air flick the still burning butt
toward a black grime curb puddle
without thought, just instinct
to smoke/blow/flick and walk away
with no clean memory stored up
for that dark day when green peas
slip off the knife for lack of honey and
bright eyes that watch me turn dim
where can I trigger a switch
to stop/breathe/think and turn
to see raw grace spurt from the street
as if I still had a chance
to eat those peas
taste that honey
see bright eyes smiling again

Jelly Babies

At the last bakery on the planet, we want
to know who dressed that baby, who made
the decisions that morning on the hat,
on the booties, and how this child would
be shaped by funky colors and fabrics
while watching the scarfing of adult crullers
and bear claws into unshaven faces, breathing
in the sugary air, hearing the counter bell
calling the next customer to a heaven baked
before the sun was discovered today and
maybe like most things, it doesn't matter
if they dressed a slouching stroller baby
in dark glasses, as if a florescent lit bakery
would be too bright for this hip infant
who looks back at us as if
we were lost wanderers from another planet,
a childless star, floating around the kids
and diapers thing, just stopping here
to drink coffee and use the bathroom
on our annual trip across the universe,
hooked on croissants of all earthly things
and seeking jelly donut asylum
to watch babies discover the world
on their own, kids who seemed born again
to help us smile, make us almost human
with their spastic jelly smears, spontaneous
jerky kicks, always demanding more and

accepting the love of strangers like us
as if the whole world was a family
of never-lost relatives who could be found
safely eating at a bakery, as we re-charged
with glazed everything at formica tables
before launching into another shaky day
in the blackholes and steel glass buildings
of this hopped up hopeful donut planet
where cool, funky jelly babies rule.

Savage Beauty

Remember that movie where a wolf
walked across a city street as if lost
in a dangerous neighborhood, a good wolf
who had to act tough, be seen as a homicidal
lone wolf who might be carrying a weapon

not understanding that anyone who saw her
in the city would be dead in their minds
would pray for a taxi to cruise by looking
for a fare to maybe take this savage beauty
to the edge of town, please, north to safety,

north to an organic bite at an outdoor cafe,
2 for 1 appetizers after this crazy city
adventure, perhaps a carafe of red wine
then a power nap with a recurring dream
of being a cool pup again, trotting to school

on one of those thunderous first days
with middle school anxiety eating at her, so
unsure of her sexuality or skills in gym class,
self-conscious about her outer coat
about her parents, who fight over little things

like boundaries and territory, a scrabbly den
of a snarling, snapping pack
always hunting hungry and thick with paranoia

and in the clear eyes of the lost urban wolf
a constant sadness

carried in each slow careful step on concrete
to be so out there, so alone, listening
for a howl to get direction, to find family, but
hearing only honks of car horns and tires
screeching to a stop, hating

every minute being out there as night
unravels in scratchy shooting stars
and she runs alone past everything,
runs until she finds her woods,
her own familiar place to hide.

Good Boy

He drives to work on auto-pilot
same route, same time every day
and in the morning he has
this simple parking lot moment
after he closes the truck door -
he opens it again for
a quick look, a final glance
a non-brain emotional compulsion
pulling his eye and heart
for a mere three seconds, a look back
as if he had forgotten top secret papers,
a back up pair of shoelaces, or
he could hear his mother's muffled voice
speaking from the mobile grave
of the dusty glove box with
her love, eternal worry and instructions
to check the lights
sit up straight today
chew his lunch slowly, eat
the crusts and crisp iceberg lettuce
of his regular Tuesday egg salad sandwich,
reminding him even in the smell of leather seats
and in the dim glow of the overhead light,
she loved him and noticed he had buckled up,
good boy,
now, double-check the lights
now, go in to work already.
Don't be late.

Armed and Dangerous

I heard on the radio they were looking
for me, described as armed and dangerous,
though grubby and hungry is more like it,
need a shower, a shave, some scrambled eggs
a nice stretch on the soft blue yoga mat
I found in the closet of the unknown single
white female's place I broke into after she left
thank god, to do whatever she does
but I'll need a nap on the Ikea couch
maybe catch up on e-mail while I wait for them
to find me, find this clean 1BR apt., a normal one
in a complex of three story look-alike buildings with
quiet neighbors, who are mostly at work
so would never see the SWAT Team
in their serious black bullet-proof vests silently
storming this place with helmets
and professional doses of hot adrenaline
pumping toward their trigger fingers, practicing
synchronous heart palpitations, signaling each
other with this-is-not-a-drill looks
that the new swat guy is trying to decipher
needing to know what to do next,
not thinking if he will or will not live
to see his daughter's birthday next week
and no one is perfect, mistakes are made
so maybe, I should unlock the door
while I shower to be safer
or will a burglar sneak in, take her ipad and go

can't trust anyone these days, but
what are the odds of that as I shave and sing
coffee dripping into a 10 cup carafe
and I don't want to be captured naked,
how embarrassing for all of us,
a classic SWAT story to be told later, how the dude
was just completely oblivious singing in the shower
when we took him down, couldn't resist like that
but we wrestled him to the tile floor, while clearing
the other rooms and it was over in like a minute, but
I know they won't even find me for awhile, so I'll
just hang out, watch Sports Center on mute
maybe go for a run later
not contact anyone, keep the music low
no stupid shit, well, no more, just
smile if anyone stops by, because after this, damn,
I might be locked away forever, go through
all kinds of bad shit,
the horror of human faces distorted by the inequities
of this american life, every kind of drug
and sick scrambled mind all locked up together
as if the right mix of guards and yard time will begin
to make sense and we'll all see the error of our ways,
and I am sorry for most everything too, like some
of those guys, but I'm also thinking
I better get those eggs, it's all good here alone
a simple peace, if only for a day,
it never lasts
she'll be home, I'll be gone
and when this mess unravels
it will be a long day.

Dead Poor

Sometimes, it's enough to go out
sit in the car, run the heater, get high
and warm the whole thing up
in the middle of winter, late at night
when the radio talks aliens and ghosts
with such conviction, they could start
a church, save me from this life
as I check mirrors, lock doors
as though a real ghost can't slip in
some other way or maybe it's me
they're talking about and I'm the alien,
a stoned scared space bug of a guy
missing people parts or feelings
or some other basic human quality
they don't need on my home planet
or could be I'm just alienated
from my family, who are upstairs
in out little apt. acting their age
and place in this world, sleeping
at the appropriate time under mounds
of goodwill and blankets
not expecting me to slip back in
with a plan of more than hope,
more than prayer, more than
maybe, maybe tomorrow will be better
kids, lying to myself
as I drift away into thin bits

of human debris, leftover
scraps of life as it should be, fading
a little more each day, as winter
pushes closer in to lick my bones
and I pop out to this cold, smoky car
to think, to try to think of what
I can do to get us in a better place
a house, a safe neighborhood
and a car that don't freeze up overnight
stranding us with wind whipping
through us like we're really thin ghosts
or some kind of aliens no one cares
about, all of us just shivering kids
who lived poor and might always
be like this, dead poor
without bus fare to get away
or even knowing what bus to take
to get there, but knowing we damn
well sure need more than a city bus
to get us out of here.

Safe Distances

One of my reasons for riding the bus
is I may chance to sit beside an Emily
Dickinson.

I like the concept of may chance
as much as I do finding a like-Emily riding
a public bus, reading something old and solid,
fully aware of the stops, knowing the next
stop offers a definite chance of something new
to be observed even while pretending to read.

Actually, a crudgy man like me may get on
or would she think board, yes, board the bus
and we lurch a bit as the bus pulls away like
they do, starting us on a simple dance together
in the chugging silence of a full bus, and what
are the chances of her being there and wondering
if I am Walt Whitman or even just Whitmanish
going uptown on a Wednesday morning for a drink.

I may be after an early lunch and she would
picture me striding through a scattering of dirty
urban pigeons on the wide avenue, wondering
what it might be like to get off and follow at a
safe distance

from this shuddering world, that keeps erupting
into sharp-edged pieces of new life, that suddenly
scream at us to take notice, take notice of the
birth of a day that can swallow us whole or laugh
aloud at the may chance approach to meeting an
Emily Dickinson on a whale of an old city bus,
both of us burying our heads in different books
at the same time while inside every single cell
celebrates the brilliant light of each other.

still life in lawn chair

there was an old guy who set out a chair
by the main road each day
to watch the world go by, fascinated
by the comings and goings, how things
did change if you waited long enough,
were crazy if you watched close enough
and he wasn't bored by the apparent boring
looked kinda simple, mindless,
and people would wave, honk,
take visitors by to see him there
as they drove in patterns he learned
sitting with a glass of tea
ball cap on, legs crossed like on older Jesus,
a tired God assigned to small towns
patient with empty gaps in traffic
when all was quiet and nothing
seemed to happen and he could think
on it a bit, say a prayer
for the health of those he had not seen
pray for mercy for nearly everyone
he had seen, listen for birds
as they did the business of birds with babies
who had to eat, who needed to fly
away, and in his steady way, as he sat
through his still life on a lawn chair, he saw
everything, all the weather, new cars,
outlaws, in-laws, babies in strollers,

kids grow up and disappear and the solemn call
of the church bell for funerals, a soundtrack
for small towns where life was life,
milk was milk, a place where whiskey
lived with prayer, laughter and ragged hope,
thick with good people who knew too much
about each other, maybe not enough
about themselves, but believed
he would be there by the road
each day, counting on him for something
they couldn't understand, not thinking
it too deep, really, just letting him sit
so still.

Dinner Invitation

From the address on the invitation,
I picture a winding road
on a hill that I'll have to coast
slowly down around curves
on a snowy evening,
trying to read faded numbers on mailboxes,
headlights behind me insisting a knowledge
of the canyon I do not have.
I want them to pass me in the soft dusk
to lead the way to a cozy house
with a full bar and chatty guests,
but they're content to sit on my bumper
and speculate on my intelligence
as I go deeper
into this tree lined canyon,
more like a lost explorer
than a not so hungry dinner guest
who will later navigate the uphill darkness
following the swishy red taillights
of other drunken guests, but
who now wonders about the long dead
city planner who knew this would happen
many nights and that I could eventually find
a stone mailbox with a red balloon
flailing a welcome through snow flurries
pointing the way to a gravel drive
of an old house they say has character

with a wide wrap-around summer porch
smoking chimney and slobbery chocolate lab
but, in the first light of this dinner invitation,
it was just another old house
in the dark woods of my antisocial imagination
and I had ten days to consider my regrets.

Oh, come on

I want to say oh, come on to the man
pitching a fit over a simple $3 parking ticket
he got for staying too long at lunch
but, he's a big, burly, bearded, hairy
all over non-teddy bear type, who may not
take kindly to my comment, well,
what adult wants to hear oh, come on,
as if he was a child, as if I was
this man's daddy and could sweep him up
in my arms, swing him around, plop him
on my shoulders for a ride around the block
to get his mind off the parking ticket
then flip him down, like Daddies do,
tickle his hairy belly as his black t-shirt
rode up his chest and just like that
everything would be good again,
and he would go home, open
his piggy bank of coins, hop on
his Harley and cruise down to the station
to pay the ticket, maybe pick me up
a six pack on the ride home, by way
of thanks, Dad, don't know what
came over me, so silly acting up
like that on Main St., at a lady just doing
her job - reminds me of the time
the airline cancelled our flight to Disney,
remember, and it all worked out

because it was raining there anyway
and we all had burgers at that strip joint
near the airport, while waiting for
the next flight, which I would tell him
I don't remember at all, buddy, only to
hear him come back with his own
oh, come on, and tease me as if
we really were or could be a family
who went to Disney via strip joints
together, and not just strangers
who pass each other by, not a word,
just a glance to see we're different
keep going, knowing, but not wanting
to admit we're so much alike.

Addicted to Lucinda Williams

I'm staying away from the throbbing house
down the block blasting Lucinda Williams
songs all night - front door open like a beacon
on hell with an obvious onion sizzle smell
oozing up the street, escaping in gasps
out doors, windows, screens and vents
flying in all directions down cracked sidewalks
across a litter-strewn street
invading my rental yard like a crazed dog
overturning a rusted red wagon
that once pulled my kid's desperate dreams
around the block, until they escaped
from this haunting midnight landscape
where I remain alone, with the low standard
of at least staying away
from houses painted the color of night,
seen in pitiful 40 watt light
through smoke stained lamp shades
hiding the smell of fear and death
set permanently in a sat out red sofa
below a framed photo of a former life
stuck on the wall like a shrine
to better times to be worshipped
with the whipped-up passion of cheap beer,
while a tv glows in the corner
with the same shows I watch every night,
trembly worried that this could be my life,

my house, if I was not so damn afraid
of becoming addicted to Lucinda Williams,
staying up all hours in a night house
that's just a neon runny egg diner for people
on drugs or worse, people who no longer
care if their creepy house has a heart
for beaten down tired working people
who can only taste this hard life now,
not sure they can get off the couch
sing along, go to Memphis
go to Sidell
go somewhere
anywhere,
find someone and find their joy.

6 mi W. of Cedar Vale
weather reported by amateur radio

Around 4:30, a retired farmer reported an observation
from the weather station on his family wheat farm

that a wind of 60 mph had blown a gust of cool air
by his place as he sat alone in his basement

sipping Folgers and monitoring things,
which he did most days now he had sold his land,

auctioned off his equipment and junk, just
keeping the house he had built with his wife, who

passed this year, leaving behind her sweetness,
the scent of rose from flowers she grew and dried

for potpourri, which he set on his radio to warm each day
rekindling his memory of her and what she would say

about wind, storms and rough times they lived through
out here west of town, where you could see it coming,

but think maybe it would miss you, like it often did,
different than the way he missed her now, feeling her

presence moving him, such a strong gust of her
turning the rooster weather vane of his rusted heart

as he sits drinking coffee by a staticky ham radio
6 mi W. of Cedar Vale, Kansas.

Happy to be the Dog

There are large dogs pulling women
around our neighborhoods and parks,
as though a new sport was invented
in the pages of a woman's magazine
that pictures model housewives or
smart singles snuggling perfectly cloned
canine buddies - fat black labs, galloping
golden retrievers, sleek, rescued greyhounds
who gleam from slick pages
with trained smiles of gnarly teeth,
and these beasts are thrilled
to be going home with the girl
panting warm puppy breath at the thought
of being hugged by these women
who giggle when they're jumped on
slobbered on and leg humped
with acceptable unfettered animal passion
by their frisky friends,
leashed to manageable control
by skinny women, who have no need
for a small sad beagle,
women who have discarded indecisive mutts
with no sense of humor, ignored
whiney dachshunds to risk danger
with a tall dark doberman
but are often iffy on the two-legged beast,
plain or whiskered, who might not take

to the lessons of a tight leash, might be
jealous of large extroverted dogs, but needy
enough to walk in the park, maybe talk,
anxious to-not-be alone,
unattached, even to a leash
willing to please, to pant, to beg
happy to be the dog, if that's what it takes.

If You Only Have 1 Day

The travel books like to be realistic
and advise you on how to spend
your time if you only have a week

or 3 days, and they're crackerjack
good editors, who in a few words
take an attitude if you linger at

the section titled if you only have
one day in Rome or Paris or Carmel,
Indiana, as if you wouldn't be there

longer, if you could, and you read
between the lines too, so it's not
just what they say, but you know

what they think about people
like you, one day people, day-
trippers on a budget, just out

for a photo of the Coliseum
a selfie at the Eiffel Tower, or
worse yet, a postcard of Carmel

yes, the one in Indiana, not
Carmel-by-the-Sea, who even
goes there, they think, especially

when life gets down to one measly
day and everyone is pulled off life
support and sent out into the world

to travel, to experience a culture,
have fun or to find a former love
who disappeared in the '60's

rumored to have become a UU
Minister in the Midwest, last known
contact was not in the middle of

Paris, browsing the Louvre, but
in Carmel, where some of you
have been, where you can eat

something real at Mudbugs and
there in the corner, quietly having
chili with a huge cinnamon roll

could be the love of your life, last
day, last chance, no time to take
an attitude or read between the

lines, just coffee and a roll
with an old friend beats the crowd
at the Mona Lisa any old day.

Despite it All

The man sitting smoking on his front step
in faded torn t-shirt and cranky pants, head
bowed to the onslaught of life and traffic
is taking a short break from his reality

thinking that one smoke will not be enough,
that 5 minutes out of that house to breathe
is like a 500 million dollar lottery win
on a day when he's a billion short in life,

with no way out of this dreary picture
and the death he is working up to is coming
torturously slow, as if the poison of his choices
was feeding through an IV one drop at a time

keeping him barely alive, just enough to work
and remember when evenings came with a chance
for relief from the honest labor of the day, when

suddenly, he hears his name shouted from inside,
as if he was needed to do something useful, to
bring his smile to the dinner table with a prayer
of thanks for this much, for a family to eat

together with a roof over their heads, not starving,
not as crazy as the neighbors or as foolish as some
who don't realize that, yeah, life's a struggle, but
it could be worse and despite it all give thanks.

Science Quiz

It's time to sit up straight
check the sharp tip of the #2
and hack that brain

as questions float through 10th
Gradeland to sit on the desk
waiting for answers about who

you are, are going to be, to be with
and what comes next, what words
will open doors that need to be

explored, and now on Friday afternoon
a pop quiz, science, every last thing
you might never know, having relied

on faith to get past the mystery, not
to understand every cell and neuron
so you take a minute

to find your own questions, close your
eyes and clearly see gray gaps
between the hard as anthracite answers

wonder if you had been home sick
the day they taught about connective
tissue, the firm strand of DNA

between science and spirit, between
data and people, the bloody heart
and the from-the-heart heart, one

of which pounds as the clock ticks, as
you hear pencils scratching out
answers and try to hear the writing

of science words like aorta, biology
and cytology, vast fields you'll never
run through to discover and learn

that not everything is easy
that thinking is not feeling
and God might have failed science

too, if he had made it to 10th grade
and met a girl, had a boyfriend
if his parents split up

for no reason too,
when he was still trying to figure
things out, bummer,

science quiz out of nowhere, so
you look for questions you know
the answers to, like, is this the end

of the world - true or false, but it's not
there, and you already know this
ain't it and tomorrow's Saturday.

What We Call a Rose

It wasn't just the crimson
perfection of the red rose

she was offering to the busy,
to the hustling, anonymous

get out of my way people
walking Michigan Avenue

on one of those colorless cloud
covered common Tuesdays

but, her crackly Mother Teresa
face glowed warm from a fire

within, that erupted when she
realized she had everything

when even nothing was enough,
so, her entire being became

what we call a smile
every cell pinging wild

inside, as she felt pure joy
that she gave away

through Eternity red roses
whose every fold and

petal invited the receiver
to a universal party

and stopped their crazy rush
for just a moment to feel

what we call grace.

Asking the neighbor to shoot his own

dog, when it yaps at 3 a.m. to alert us
that another damn star fell from the sky
and he thinks, in his infinite canine wisdom
that the planet is no longer safe, or

that's the grizzled gist of it, he goes on and on
and that's what I'm able to gather as I sit
in my supposed-to-be-quiet night kitchen
translating dog talk into human words

I can understand. When I call, I hold the
phone to the open window, so his dog
can speak directly to him, maybe whine
and grovel about please let me inside.

Brave dog. My neighbor owns the same gun
I do and I ask if he is short on bullets or balls,
he laughs and says how ya doin', as if
we were both asleep, sharing a bad dream.

Thing is, I like the middle of the night when
most people are sleeping and as my mother
says 'nothin good ever happens, yada yada,
that's when you was born.' She talks like that.

This time of night most stuff closes down
traffic shuts itself up and if the dog don't yap
it's an entirely different world with a lost in
space silence, almost the peace I think I need.

I want to wake up to a life like spring Sundays
with no hangover, no phone, nothin to bother,
windows open to songbirds, a fresh breeze
pushing a few fat clouds around as if God found

the original plan for paradise, dusted it off,
realized dogs barking all night was a mistake
only meant for a few assholes. Ah, he let 'em in !
Quiet. Now, it's just me.

Arriving at Church an Hour Before God

Arriving at church an hour before God
is scheduled to appear amongst the faithful,
I am surprised at the number
of early risers who sit alone or in pairs,
in carefully staked out wooden pews
that allow a physical buffer for the spirit,
space from each other,
from each other's thoughts and prayers
space that absorbs
the totality of their silence
like a saintly vacuum for everyday sins
and worse
until, not knowing the start time,
I intrude, squeak open the doors
let them bang shut
walk across oak plank floorboards
creaking as if I had awakened them to yawn
out old testaments of genuflections
in the echo of this mostly empty church
turning every head slowly toward me
in the reverence of withholding judgment
until they are certain I am not him
they do not know me,
who could never be him
the one who is always there for them
not making noise
not smiling the wrong smile, like me

with an embarrassed grin that begs forgiveness
a mere mortal's smile,
not that beatific, peaceful countenance
of the venerable church custodian
who turns on the heat each winter morning
before sitting down to bask in the gratitude
of the daily Mass holy ones.
Let us Pray.

Belly Crawl

Before there were soldiers
trained to belly crawl
under razor wire

there were babies
learning to crawl

and once they had it
could always get low
to scoot across cold tile

to silently creep
inch by inch, holding

their soft breath, simple
miracles, ready to slip
under the concertina wire

of kitchen chair and table
legs, where their father sat

worrying about everything
never suspecting a commando
crawling in his house

and if God could end this
endless war of life

right before the child
tickled her father's bare
dangling foot,

the world might miss
another moment of love

it so desperately needs.

Half Crazy

It doesn't matter which half is the crazy side
of a person to an un-trained observer,
as long as we get to deal with the calm
rational response side when we confront
the beer belly of sanity over a small thing
like a lap dog on a leash,
squatting in the light of an indifferent moon,
a sad crescent seeing the dog poop
daily, on the edge of my lawn,
without a scoop in the meaty hand
of the fat guy who holds a red leather leash
clipped to the studded collar of this lame
little fur-ball mama's dog, who just wants
relief and is into routine, like many of us
so, same lawn day after damn day -
mine, and something about the guy's
t-shirt tells me he drinks Bud,
not light, and he is a proud dog-loving
tax-paying, flag-waving American
who won't understand my half-sane side
as I approach him smiling
with a doggie biscuit and gun.

Blessings

Toward the end of our last visit together
you gave me a blessing in that vague
secular way, for the universe to shower
me with love, all good things and heaps
of healthy, peaceful vibes, which it did,
thanks, in that quiet as our best angels
way and I felt so open, so safe, joyous
and uninhibited that I threw a party,
drank some seriously blessed wine
and ale made by the good monks,
ingested what can be described as other
good stuff, and now I can't remember
what happened, but from that night on
I've misplaced that basic blessing
as though I had passed out on that fat
soft chair by the big world-is-passing-by
window and it fell out of my pocket
with loose change and into the cushions
or rolled on the floor, and the dog licked
it up, she eats anything and has been running
crazy slobbery circles of chasing her tail
with good vibes, and while hungover
I've looked everywhere for that damn
blessing and maybe I'm looking too hard,
it could be right there losing power amongst

house plants or suffocating while fighting
its way out of the party's plastic trash bag
of lost dreams, but I can't touch it or it me
so I'm wondering what it would take now
to have a do-over blessing on my life again.

Fingers in the Bowl

My mind tasted chocolate before my fingers
hit the bowl, triggered by memory, by anticipation
of licking up the sticky dark sweet,

having done this every time we made a sheet cake
for my birthday, knowing, even if the oven fails
we'll slurp the uncooked batter like starving lovers

meeting in the kitchen after midnight, aching
from our bed, restless, needy for something not
so raw as each other,

like food that comforts and refills our memory
of what we were like as children who knew real love
who could by instinct and smell find mothers

in an afternoon kitchen, smoking, whisking
a store-bought cake mix in a pink fiesta-ware bowl
without a thought they were missing something

more important than us. We would wait for the cake
to rise while licking electric mixer tongs. I still wait
for cakes to cook. To cool. To frost. To levitate

off the granite counter and sail around the kitchen
in search of a single cherry of simple care, looking for
pecans to crush and scatter in a random pattern

of perfection before billions of desperate fingers
dive into our mixing bowl planet to mindlessly lick
and consume it, to nearly wipe it out, leaving

just a trace for the kids, who smell something
they are told had once been so sweet, so good
we had to have it, had to have it all.

Goodwill

Choosing a goofy knit winter hat
from a discard bin of free, donated
giveaways at Goodwill, I shake it
out hard looking to the linoleum
floor for unmentionables falling
from any previous heads
that wore the hat, look carefully
into the orange and green yarn
for evidence of dirt and bug
in case they didn't wash it -
that would be an official bummer -
nits in a knit cap
bug eggs hatching
in my floppy
ear-flapped life and my warm
head incubating a litter of cute
micro-bug babies who crawl
inside my ear canals, setting
out from each side to find
siblings in the damn middle
of my head to bug party hard
and loud, drunken dancing
around my brain, yucky bug
puke oozing in and softening
my mind from an infestation
this winter - scary stuff -
these unspeakable things

happen and people go crazy
by February and no one knows
why, so I just ask the lady
at the counter if they wash
all the free stuff and
she tells me *everything,
everything* with a smile
and her kind eyes get inside
me the way my 2nd grade
teacher did when she told me
everything happens for a reason
and not to worry so much
and other stuff I forgot, so
still don't know, but I do know
I need a hat and have no
money, so I thank her
for washing, for everything,
put on my new hat
pull down the cool ear flaps
let the tie strings dangle
because even I have limits
and I give her a free smile
and head on out the door.

Roughed Up

*From an Art in America interview
with artist Eileen Quinn, March 2011*

She was feeling stuck (def. - unmoving; unable to move)
thought some violence might help -
she pauses to suck down smoke
and as I watch taking notes
the pause sits smoking on a pigeon bombed ledge
of this high-rise, double-paned windows
sealed tight and sound-proof
until her laugh emits remnants of smoke
mixed with wisps of memory we both see
floating there for her to identify
knowing she has it in her
it will always touch her
and I think she's bypassed dust to become
cells of smoke that are reciting history
for me to record in pencil, wondering if I can
use this virgin eraser to make things right again;
the violence, I prompt her, to shatter the pause
and she jumps as though I had knuckle
rapped the glass from inside -
uh, yes, of course, violence is the point
isn't it, she says, lighting up again, explaining
we worked our way up to it and around
it like sailors finding skinny white legs
on rough seas - that was us then,
push, slap, pinch, back-hand smacks,
spank, burn, cut

little dark things that happen after drinking
binges made our skin thick colorless slabs
with fun house faces we didn't recognize
and thus, she says, her word, thus, fucking thus
I guess we got scared, angry we were so stuck,
back-handed smacks could not rattle our muse, so
started punching each other, took turns,
silly, I know, maybe crazy
and we would wake up so sore and take polaroids
of the bruises, while they were fresh and ugly,
don't know why, but people looked at them
wanted to see the worst
the close-ups of body parts
distorted arms, boobs, dribbles of blood
hell, the whole thing was sick
us and them and hair —
we'd find snatches of hair in our hands
and we'd show the polaroids around
get some money and that my friend
she said, smushing out the butt
that was what got us unstuck
and able to paint again.

It doesn't get better

We feel at home in the suburbs. It
seems stainless. Meditatively empty.

No one points out my real sins
as we find space for them in

storage sheds, plastic containers,
well organized garage shelving,

stacks of sins stowed in a cool
dry and nicely finished basement.

We need every sq.ft. of forgiveness
and this nice half acre of blessing.

City people focus on our lawns, the
greenness of life with straight

edges. The lawns do keep us busy
most of the year and in winter, we

dream of wild prairie grasses burning
in the night. In the breakfast nook on

winter mornings, we sip green tea
while warming our car seats.

It doesn't get better, we think,
while allowing our actual better

angels to live in the city, ride a
train out Sundays to comfort us,

to haul our doubts away in a
reusable bag to abandon on

the train, while we take yoga
class, breathe deep and repeat

our mantra: It's all good. It's
all good. It's all good.

Thin Crust

What if your last 21 pizzas
were all delivered in the last 3 weeks
of your life, one-a-day
beginning with a thick crust supreme
and gradually becoming less each day
until your last pizza is a small thin crust
cheese brought by a skinny teen
who is shocked to see you
apparently dying in a recliner
while daily calling for pizza,
with a liter of cold diet cola
to be delivered
to your dimly lit, trashed apartment
where a slice of sausage sticks to the carpet
and the reek of rotting uneaten mushrooms
is mixed with your daily crusts
amidst a scattering of twenty empty boxes
and piles of pepper and cheese packets
and the kid takes it all in,
looks at you, then quickly away
sick at how real life can be
trying to grasp how long you could live
like this, with barely a pulse
but, still thinking pizza
which he had in a warming bag,
not sure where to set it down,
afraid to get too close

as if all this could be caused by pizza
some mad obsession with pepperoni
and you tell him *anywhere*
the money's on the table there
and the kid does his job
thinking - is he alright
smiling - forget the tip
asking - *do you need, want extra cheese ?*
as if that was all it would take to save you.

Perishables

I must have been dreaming
in a crowded arid land, woke
up thirsty, hearing a whistle

in the night which sounded
like a train switching tracks
before rolling south carrying

tons of wheat to another grain
elevator and I thought
hello, what is going on here

why move so much food in the
middle of the night, why pretend
we all control our pantry

filling our shelves, stocking
enough per house to feed a village
with jars, cans, frozen everything

to save non-perishables, like us,
for a day that might never arrive

never looks like
the brown face of a perishable
child with questioning eyes

her hands never getting close
to pulling a pewter pantry
knob to open and see what

she's out of, what to add
to her weekly shopping list
maybe something sweet

hello, what is going on now
what happened to that moment
was it just a blink after the dream

when we knew we had enough.

Enough for today. Enough to
split into sharable portions, to
toss a leftover slice to my dog

who is listening as I open a
white styrofoam box and see
half a meal uneaten

because an inflated portion size
was too large for one meal, after
appetizers and drinks, laughter

and no, there is no room, did
not save room for dessert
as yummy as they appear.

I think I've had enough, thanks.
Enough for years, enough for a
full line of drive-through folks

I'll see at the gym tomorrow
walking on treadmills or spinning
their way toward lunch, listening

to podcasts about fat babies, did
I hear that right, fat babies in
photos posing as animals

we love, we love 'em all, the
babies and mothers and bears
who store up food for a long

winter in a homey cave, dreaming
of more, of more salmon for bear
cubs, so cute, this wonderful life

we live, this endless life we shop
for on-line finding other non-
perishables to compete with, for

the best and brightest, knowing
there is a continent somewhere
full of perishable babies, adorable

kids with desperate mommies
who count the days they have
with their loved ones and know

it is not, could never be enough.

Discovery Adventure Wonder

Waking in an unfamiliar bed
you gotta be up for adventure,
know it's happening when
you open your eyes, naked
in a dark unknown house
listening for pre-dawn sounds,
for hints of a possessive cat,
of an old clock ticking away
a quiet life, sounds
of a cold truck chugging up
the street below this second story
room with a classic old house smell
shallow breathing from her
beside me - was it a party, a bar, work
a date, a dating site meet up and we hit
it off with our keen childlike sense
of wonder, open to discovering new people
and cool places like this bedroom
and it would be good to be
one of the new people for a change
people open to seeing what a new day
like this might bring, what day
it might be, so I might slip out
do the right thing
find coffee, rifle a medicine cabinet
for ibuprofen, damn, and of course
I need to find a toilet, but know

I could bump into a kid or
another stranger in the hall with a face
of questions, his own look of wonder
at meeting me like this
too early for that
or to meet a small yapping dog
family members, roommates
who dislike stranger in the house surprises
and downstairs maybe an old man
in faded boxers watching tv weather
in his vinyl recliner, I get that
so I'll wait
for these exciting discoveries, roll
over to my edge of her bed
close my eyes
review new dreams, think of fresh
options for mornings like this,
try to piece the night together
from there to here, from no one
to her, driving or walking
maybe a taxi, uber, a ride from a friend
whatever, I know this: I'm alive
love this glorious not-knowing situation
of life that tickles me
with delicious chunks of night
to discover and touch new hearts
accepting it may not all be good
I could be the nightmare in her morning
or I could find a frontier intersection
of our hearts, a simple hook-up

so years from now we'll forget
even this craggy wake-up of heads buried
in average pillows and this warm bed
with a comforter that reeks of normal,
of comfort, a small clue of a larger life
that has family and breakfast, posed photos
stories of school, crazy uncles
and she's a good sleeper,
indications of a clear conscience,
simple contentment or a drug problem,
so God be with me if she wakes
today having forgotten she brought me
home, or I her
I don't know, but I'm excited to see
what comes next, being brave
I'll find a bathroom, make life awake noises
eyes wide open, take that next step to reveal
or unravel this achy adventurous life.

Too Early to Cry

Too early to cry, she thought
as she put on water for a quiet
black breakfast tea

that would float in a mug like a resort
guest, staring at cracks in her sky
painted kitchen ceiling, waiting

to swim across her stubbly tongue
to be swallowed sip by sip, but
she let her tea just sit until cooled

to a season shifting temp, getting ready,
still too early she told herself, waiting
for the change,

for a new day to crack that sky
and the next season to begin,
until, she set aside her teacup

brewed a bully pot of proud little
jamaican coffee beans, thinking
what she had been thinking all along,

as her second thick ceramic white mug
of black took hold of her warm memories
of him, lifted them dancing in wispy steam

to that same cracked sky before a new
pink sun streaked like a shy child god
through her night sink window,

before she was quite ready to listen
for the birds, to hear the first notes
of a hungry song from the first robin

of spring, who somehow knew to sing
the same song every year, the same joy
she heard when he was still alive

and shared this first morning ritual with her,
listening together for this simple sign
that signaled such new life

that it moved them both to smile,
and was their sign that it was now time
and was okay to cry at the wonder of it all.

This Song

This is not the story
of my life unless
you are in it
so much
it could be the
made up story
of you, of all
of us and others
we never knew
who came before
including you know
who and probably
who came after
and it grabs your
face to start, so
much light we see
what can happen
next, discover sun,
stars, the universe
then a juicy middle
a slow feast of life
with cheese, wine
sweet desserts
endless talk
bad words
laughter, that's what
we remember, joy

as we sip wine
and afternoon
stretches like a cat
who reminds us
of a gentle sunset
when we're hungry
for something to hold,
as we see what
is left of this day
but, excited for all
we have and we have
each other,
not alone
we know things now,
know how
this song just goes
on and on and on.

Joe McKenzie grew up in Philadelphia, went to colleges in Pennsylvania, Kansas and Colorado. He enjoyed a long career in libraries, while writing as many poems as would come, retiring as Director of the Salina Public Library. He has been active in the community and continues to volunteer. He has been commissioned to write and read a series of poems on Andy Warhol's electric chair paintings at the Salina Art Center. He was a New Voice Award winner as part of the Annual Spring Poetry Reading Series in Salina, Ks. He lives with his wife, Mary Lou, in Salina, visits his granddaughters in Kansas City often and enjoys traveling to see his son and daughter-in-law in France and his family on the east coast.

www.ingramcontent.com/pod-product-compliance
Lightning Source LLC
Chambersburg PA
CBHW020124130526
44591CB00032B/521